U.S. HISTORY IN REVIEW

The Spanish-American War

Emmett Martin

Enslow Publishing

Please visit our website, www.enslow.com. For a free color catalog of all our high-quality books, call toll free 1-800-398-2504 or fax 1-877-980-4454.

Portions of this work were originally authored by Marie Roesser and published as *The Spanish-American War.* All new material this edition authored by Emmett Martin.

Cataloging-in-Publication Data
Names: Martin, Emmett.
Title: The Spanish-American War / Emmett Martin.
Description: Buffalo, NY : Enslow Publishing, 2027. | Series: U.S. History in review | Includes glossary.
Identifiers: ISBN 9781978547162 (pbk.) | ISBN 9781978547179 (library bound) | ISBN 9781978547186 (ebook)
Subjects: LCSH: Spanish-American War, 1898–Juvenile literature.
Classification: LCC E715.M327 2027 | DDC 973.89–dc23

Published in 2027 by
Enslow Publishing
2544 Clinton Street
Buffalo, NY 14224

Designer: Leslie Taylor
Interior layout: Tanya Dellaccio Keeney
Editor: Therese Shea

Photo credits: Series art (grunge flag) Andrey Kuzmin/Shutterstock.com; series art (stamp icon) Stocker_team/Shutterstock.com; series art (font) santstock/Shutterstock.com; series art (swash) BUTENKOV ALEKSEI/Shutterstock.com; cover Courtesy of The National Museum of History/Flickr.com; p. 5 https://upload.wikimedia.org/wikipedia/commons/2/2b/San_Juan_Hill_by_Kurz_and_Allison.JPG; p. 7 https://upload.wikimedia.org/wikipedia/commons/8/86/Cuban_soldiers%2C_1898.jpg; p. 9 (top) https://upload.wikimedia.org/wikipedia/commons/e/e2/McKinley_sworn_in.jpeg; p. 9 (bottom) https://upload.wikimedia.org/wikipedia/commons/3/30/McKinley_%28cropped%29.jpg; p. 11 https://upload.wikimedia.org/wikipedia/commons/d/dc/USS_Maine_entering_Havana_harbor_HD-SN-99-01929.JPEG; p. 13 (top) https://upload.wikimedia.org/wikipedia/commons/8/83/Wreck_of_the_U.S.S._Maine%2C_ca._1898_-_NARA_-_512929.jpg; p. 13 (bottom) https://upload.wikimedia.org/wikipedia/commons/e/e8/World98.jpg; p. 15 https://upload.wikimedia.org/wikipedia/commons/1/1d/Spanish_troops_leaving_Mayagüez,_Puerto_Rico,_to_engage_the_American_forces_at_Hormiguero,_Puerto_Rico,_08-10-1898_-_NARA_-_533437.tiff; p. 17 https://upload.wikimedia.org/wikipedia/commons/8/8e/USS_Olympia_art_NH_91881-KN_cropped.jpg; p. 19 (top) https://upload.wikimedia.org/wikipedia/commons/c/cd/RoughRiders.jpeg; p. 19 (bottom) https://upload.wikimedia.org/wikipedia/commons/7/7d/Col_roosevelt_rough_rider.jpg; p. 20 https://upload.wikimedia.org/wikipedia/commons/3/3f/Liberators_of_Cuba.jpg; p. 21 Heritage Image Partnership Ltd./Alamy Images; p. 23 https://upload.wikimedia.org/wikipedia/commons/1/1f/Combate_en_Santiago_de_Cuba%2C_1898.jpg; p. 25 https://upload.wikimedia.org/wikipedia/commons/2/2b/John_Hay_signs_Treaty_of_Paris%2C_1899.JPG; p. 27 (top) https://upload.wikimedia.org/wikipedia/commons/2/23/Manila646_1899.jpg; p. 27 (bottom) https://upload.wikimedia.org/wikipedia/commons/f/fd/Utah_Battery_San_Juan_Bridge.jpeg; p. 29 https://upload.wikimedia.org/wikipedia/commons/2/22/Theodore_Roosevelt_by_John_Singer_Sargent%2C_1903.jpg.

Printed in the United States of America

CPSIA compliance information: Batch #CSENS27: For further information, contact Enslow Publishing, New York, New York, at 1-800-398-2504.

Contents

Words in the glossary appear in ***bold*** *the first time they are used in the text.*

War with Spain

The Spanish-American War was one of the shortest wars in history. It took place in 1898. After the war, Cuba was independent, or free, from Spain's rule. The United States gained land in **Latin America** and in the western Pacific Ocean. Read on to learn more about this war.

Learn More

The United States became known as a world power after defeating Spain in 1898.

Before the War

In 1895, Cubans began a fight for independence from Spain. Cuba had been a **colony** of Spain since 1511. Spanish leaders forced Cuban **rebels** into camps. Thousands died from illness, hunger, and poor conditions in these camps.

Cuban soldiers, 1898

Learn More

U.S. newspapers showed Cubans suffering greatly in the camps, called *reconcentrados*. This made Americans want to help the Cubans.

Some Americans **invested** in businesses in Cuba at that time. The United States sold goods to Cuba and bought goods from Cuba too. The fighting upset trade and cost Americans money. This was another reason why some Americans wanted to get **involved** in the fighting in Cuba.

McKinley (middle) is sworn in as U.S. president

Learn More

In 1897, William McKinley became president. At first, he didn't want the United States to act in Cuba.

President McKinley sent the USS *Maine* to help protect, or guard, American citizens and U.S. interests in Cuba. But on February 15, 1898, an **explosion** sank the ship, killing more than 260 people on board. The cause of the blast was unknown, but many Americans blamed Spain.

USS *Maine* in Havana Harbor, Cuba

Learn More

In 1976, a U.S. Navy report said that a coal fire on the *Maine* likely caused the explosion.

"Remember the Maine"

Many Americans were quick to place the blame for the *Maine's* explosion on Spain. "Remember the Maine!" was their cry for war. President McKinley sent a secret note to Spain calling for total independence for Cuba.

Learn More

On April 11, McKinley asked Congress to use U.S. armed forces to end the fighting between the government of Spain and the people of Cuba.

USS *Maine* after the explosion

863,956 WORLDS CIRCULATED YESTERDAY — The World. — 863,956 WORLDS CIRCULATED YESTERDAY

"Circulation Books Open to All."

NEW YORK, THURSDAY, FEBRUARY 17, 1898.

MAINE EXPLOSION CAUSED BY BOMB OR TORPEDO?

Capt. Sigsbee and Consul-General Lee Are in Doubt---The World Has Sent Special Tug, With Submarine Divers, to Havana to Find Out---Lee Asks for an Immediate Court of Inquiry---260 Men Dead.

IN A SUPPRESSED DESPATCH TO THE STATE DEPARTMENT, THE CAPTAIN SAYS THE ACCIDENT WAS MADE POSSIBLE BY AN ENEMY.

Dr. E. C. Pendleton, Just Arrived from Havana, Says He Overheard Talk There of a Plot to Blow Up the Ship---Capt. Zalinski, the Dynamite Expert, and Other Experts Report to The World that the Wreck Was Not Accidental---Washington Officials Ready for Vigorous Action if Spanish Responsibility Can Be Shown---Divers to Be Sent Down to Make Careful Examinations.

THE WHOLE STORY OF THE DISASTER TOLD IN A FEW WORDS.

War Declared

Spain stopped **negotiations** and **declared** war on the United States on April 24, 1898. The war was fought mostly in the Caribbean. It was also fought in the Philippines in Southeast Asia. The Philippines was a Spanish colony at that time.

Learn More

Before declaring war on Spain on April 25, 1898, the United States promised not to take control of Cuba.

Spanish soldiers in Puerto Rico, 1898

First Battle

Commodore George Dewey of the U.S. Navy was ordered to "capture or destroy the Spanish fleet," which was in Philippine waters. On May 1, 1898, Dewey led the American ships into Manila Bay, destroying the Spanish Pacific fleet. About 11,000 American soldiers arrived in the Philippines by the end of July 1898.

Learn More

U.S. forces took control of the capital of the Philippines—Manila—by the end of August 1898.

Battle of Manila Bay

The Cuban Conflict

U.S. Navy ships were sent to Cuba. Some stopped Spanish navy ships from escaping the harbor of the city of Santiago de Cuba. The U.S. Army sent a force to fight on land too. Some Americans felt so strongly about the war that they **volunteered** to fight.

Rough Riders

Learn More

The Rough Riders were a group of volunteer cavalry, or soldiers on horseback, with the U.S. Army in Cuba. Future president Theodore Roosevelt was their leader.

Theodore Roosevelt

The Spanish army had hilltop positions around the city of Santiago de Cuba. U.S. land forces aimed to take these and gain control of the city. On July 1, Americans won two battles to gain the city: the Battle of San Juan Hill and the Battle of El Caney.

Learn More

U.S. Army **regiments** called Buffalo Soldiers, made up of Black soldiers, stood out for their bravery during the Spanish-American War.

On July 3, 1898, the Spanish navy tried to escape the harbor of Santiago de Cuba. Their ships took fire from the waiting U.S. Navy. They were either destroyed or unable to sail on. On July 17, Spanish soldiers **surrendered** Santiago de Cuba. This ended the major fighting of the war.

Learn More

In June 1898, the U.S. Navy took control of the island of Guam, a Spanish colony in the western Pacific Ocean. The people there had not heard about the war.

Spanish ships in the harbor of Santiago de Cuba

Peace Agreement

On October 1, 1898, officials from Spain and the United States met in France. On December 10, the countries signed a peace agreement called the Treaty of Paris. Cuba received independence. Spain gave Guam and Puerto Rico to the United States.

Learn More

In all, fighting in the Spanish-American War took place over about 10 weeks.

President McKinley decided the Philippines would become a U.S. territory. The United States paid Spain $20 million for the Philippines, which is made up of over 7,600 islands. Many in the United States were against taking control of the Philippines.

Learn More

The people of the Philippines fought the United States for independence in a war from 1899 to 1902. They gained independence in 1946.

U.S. soldiers during the Philippine-American War

A Different Fight

The Spanish-American War was a few months, but many died—including more than 2,000 U.S. soldiers and 15,000 Spanish soldiers. Most died from diseases such as **typhoid fever**, not from fighting. Efforts began to study and fight these diseases. This short war had long effects on the United States and the world.

Learn More

Theodore Roosevelt was called a hero after the Spanish-American War. He became vice president in 1901 and then president when McKinley was killed in September 1901.

A Timeline of the Spanish-American War

1898

February 15
An explosion sinks the USS *Maine* in Havana Harbor.

April 24
Spain declares war on the United States.

April 25
The United States declares war on Spain.

May 1
The U.S. Navy defeats the Spanish in Manila Bay in the Philippines.

July 1
American forces win the Battle of San Juan Hill and the Battle of El Caney.

July 3
The U.S. Navy defeats the Spanish navy near Cuba.

July 17
Spanish soldiers surrender Santiago de Cuba.

October 1
Peace talks between Spain and the United States begin in France.

December 10
Spain and the United States sign the Treaty of Paris.

Glossary

colony: A piece of land under the control of another country.

commodore: The name for a captain in the U.S. Navy who commands more than one ship.

declare: To say something officially.

explosion: A sudden release of energy that can cause destruction.

invest: To spend money on something to earn more money.

involve: To become part of something.

Latin America: The Americas south of the United States.

negotiation: The act of coming to an agreement.

rebel: One who fights to overthrow a government.

regiment: A military unit made up of smaller military units.

surrender: To officially give up.

typhoid fever: A dangerous illness caused by a bacterium that spreads through food or water.

volunteer: To offer service without being asked. Also, someone who does this.

For More Information

Books

Henzel, Cynthia Kennedy. *The War Encyclopedia*. Minneapolis, MN: Encyclopedias, 2024.

Lake, Theia. *Buffalo Soldiers*. Buffalo, NY: PowerKids Press, 2024.

Website

The Spanish-American War
www.ducksters.com/history/us_1800s/spanish-american_war.php
Review a short history of the war and take a quiz.

Publisher's note to educators and parents: *Our editors have carefully reviewed these websites to ensure that they are suitable for students. Many websites change frequently, however, and we cannot guarantee that a site's future contents will continue to meet our high standards of quality and educational value. Be advised that students should be closely supervised whenever they access the internet.*

Index